W9-BAH-909

Symbols of American Freedom

Ellis Island

by Hilarie Staton

Series Consultant: Jerry D. Thompson,
Regents Professor of History,
Texas A&M International University

CHELSEA
CLUBHOUSE
An Imprint of Chelsea House Publishers

Chelsea Clubhouse
An imprint of Chelsea House Publishers
132 West 31st Street
New York NY 10001

Library of Congress Cataloging-in-Publication Data
    Staton, Hilarie.
      Ellis Island / by Hilarie Staton.
    p. cm. — (Symbols of American freedom)
    Includes index.
    ISBN 978-1-60413-519-0
    1. Ellis Island Immigration Station (N.Y. and N.J.)—Juvenile literature.
    2. United States—Emigration and immigration—History—Juvenile literature.
    3. New York (N.Y.)—Buildings, structures, etc.—Juvenile literature. I. Title. II. Series.
  JV6484.S736 2009
  304.8'73—dc22
                                              2009012067

Chelsea Clubhouse books are available at special discounts when purchased in bulk quantities for businesses, associations, institutions, or sales promotions. Please call our Special Sales Department in New York at (212) 967-8800 or (800) 322-8755.

You can find Chelsea Clubhouse on the World Wide Web at http://www.chelseahouse.com

Developed for Chelsea House by RJF Publishing LLC (www.RJFpublishing.com)
Text and cover design by Tammy West/Westgraphix LLC
Maps by Stefan Chabluk
Photo research by Edward A. Thomas
Index by Nila Glikin

Photo Credits: 5: © Onne van der Wal/Corbis; 6: Library of Congress LC-DIG-ggbain-30546; 8: Tetra Images; 11: © Bettmann/CORBIS; 15, 32: Getty Images; 16: The Granger Collection, New York; 18: Library of Congress LC USZ62-62880; 21: Library of Congress LC-USZ62-7386; 22, 31, 34: AP/Wide World Photos; 23: National Park Service; 24: Photography Collection, Miriam and Ira D. Wallach Division of Art, Prints and Photographs, The New York Public Library, Astor, Lenox and Tilden Foundations; 27: Wisconsin Historical Society; 30: Library of Congress LC-USZ62-52584; 33: Time Life Pictures/Getty Images; 37: Ambient Images; 39: agefotostock/Axiom Photographic Agency; 41: © Ted Horowitz/CORBIS; 42: agefotostock/Superstock.

Printed and bound in the United States of America

Bang RJF 10 9 8 7 6 5 4 3 2 1

This book is printed on acid-free paper.

All links and Web addresses were checked and verified to be correct at the time of publication. Because of the dynamic nature of the Web, some addresses and links may have changed since publication and may no longer be valid.

Note: Quotations in the text are used essentially as originally written. In some cases, spelling, punctuation, and the like have been modernized to aid student understanding.

Table of Contents

Words that are defined in the Glossary are in **bold** type the first time they appear in the text.

Ellis Island: Symbol of Hope and Tears

Ellis Island is a small island in New York Harbor. It is close to New York City and to New Jersey. It is also close to another small island, Liberty Island, where the Statue of Liberty stands. Although it is small, Ellis Island has played a very large role in American history. Between 1892 and 1924, it was the most important place where **immigrants** entered the United States. Immigrants are people who move to a new country to live permanently. More than 12 million immigrants came through Ellis Island during those years. This was almost three-quarters of all the immigrants entering the United States at that time. Today, more than 100 million Americans have at least one **ancestor** who came through Ellis Island.

The people who came through Ellis Island, and other immigrants as well, played a big part in making the United States the country it is today. Many of these people simply

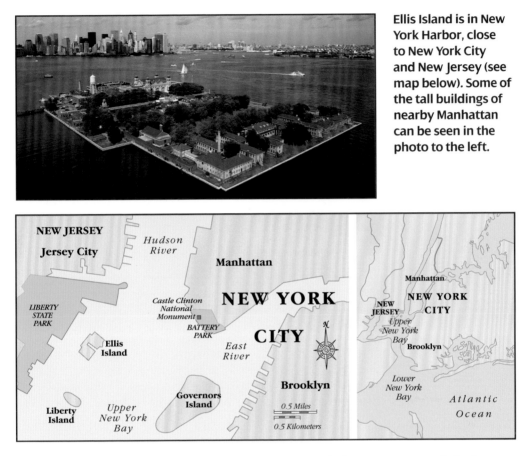

Ellis Island is in New York Harbor, close to New York City and New Jersey (see map below). Some of the tall buildings of nearby Manhattan can be seen in the photo to the left.

worked hard to make things the country needed. Some started their own businesses and made them successful. Some became important scientists or inventors. Some created great works of art or music, or helped create movies that millions of Americans have enjoyed. In these and other ways, immigrants and their families have helped the United States to grow and be successful.

Arriving in New York Harbor

Immigrants usually came to the United States by ship in the late 1800s and early 1900s. Many of them came from Europe and spent a week—or sometimes much more—in crowded ships to cross the Atlantic Ocean.

Carrying their belongings, immigrants arrive at Ellis Island at the end of a long sea voyage.

When they entered New York Harbor, one of the first things they saw was the Statue of Liberty. To these immigrants, the statue was a **symbol** of the United States and of the freedom and opportunity they hoped to find in their new country.

Ellis Island was different. Some saw it as an island of hope, but others called it an island of tears. Why these opposite feelings? Immigrants had many hopes for their new life in the United States. They hoped for a better job, an education for their children, enough to eat, and a chance to own

Max Factor (1877–1938)

Max Factor was born in Lodz, Poland. In 1904, he, his wife, and their three children entered the United States through Ellis Island. They went to St. Louis, Missouri, where he sold perfumes and creams at the 1904 World's Fair. A few years later, they moved to Hollywood, where he began doing makeup for movie actors. He invented new ways to make actors look better on film. Soon after, he began selling his makeup to the public. Over the years, he invented many new products, such as false eyelashes and the eyebrow pencil. Max Factor brand makeup is still very popular today.

In Their Own Words

End of the Journey

Edward Corsi came to the United States with his family in 1907. He wrote about what it was like in his book *In the Shadow of Liberty: The Chronicles of Ellis Island*:

> "The steamer *Florida*, fourteen days out of Naples, filled to capacity [completely full] with sixteen hundred natives of Italy had weathered one of the worst storms in our captain's memory; and glad we were, both children and grown-ups, to leave the open sea and come at last [into New York Harbor].... Passengers all about us were crowded together at the rail.... Mothers and fathers lifted their babies so that they too could see, off to the left, the Statue of Liberty."

their own land. And over time, many of them did make a better life for themselves in their new country.

But the immigrants arriving in New York had fears as well. They were worried about what might happen on Ellis Island. Many cried because they feared that the U.S. government **inspectors** would send them or someone in their family back to the country they had just left. They did not want to go back because they had nothing to return to. Often, they had sold everything to pay for their trip. Some were also afraid of what they would find after they left Ellis Island. Most immigrants did not speak English. They didn't know how they would fit into a new country with a different language and different way of life from what they were used to.

Changing Times

In 1924, American immigration laws changed. The U.S. government took steps to reduce the number of immigrants it allowed into the United States. Ellis Island continued as an **immigration station**, but mostly it was a **detention center**, where certain people were held by the government.

The Main Building on Ellis Island is now a museum that tells the story of immigrants who came to the United States to start a new life.

In Their Own Words

Not Going Home

At least at first, life was hard for many new immigrants. But many found jobs, learned English, and began to live better than they had before. Adam Paczkowski, who came from Poland and entered the United States through Ellis Island, wrote a letter in 1906 to a relative in Poland about his life in the new country:

> "I wish you to come to America...because up to the present I am doing very well here, and I have no intention of going [back] to our country, because in our country I experienced only misery and poverty, and here I live better than a lord in my country."

Making Islands

Ellis Island started out as a very small island of about 3 acres (1.2 hectares), but it was made larger over the years. In fact, today it is actually three islands. They are all joined together and seem to be one island. Each time Ellis Island was made bigger, first a wooden **seawall** was built deep into the harbor. Then the area between the island and the wall was filled with stones, dirt, and other material. Over time, Ellis Island grew from one small island to three connected islands that totaled more than 27 acres (11 hectares) and had 33 buildings.

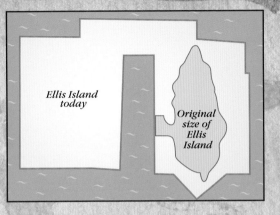

Ellis Island today

Original size of Ellis Island

This map compares the original size of Ellis Island (shown in green) with its size today.

Finally, Ellis Island was closed in 1954. It was never sold, though, and in 1965, it became part of the Statue of Liberty National Monument.

In 1982, the Statue of Liberty-Ellis Island Foundation began raising money to **restore** both places. When it asked Americans to donate (that is, to give) money to restore Ellis Island, it reminded them that this was where, in many cases, their ancestors had arrived in the United States. It found that Ellis Island was a powerful symbol to all Americans. It was a symbol of the hopes and fears that all immigrants had as they left their old countries and moved to a new, unknown life.

In 1990, the Ellis Island Immigration Museum opened in the restored Main Building. The museum tells the story of American immigrants: those who went through Ellis Island and also those who entered the United States at other locations and other times. Today, more than 2 million people a year take ferries to visit the museum at Ellis Island.

Immigration Creates a Need

During the early 1800s, the **population** of the United States grew slowly. Between 1820 and 1840, fewer than 1 million immigrants arrived. Most of them left countries in Northern and Western Europe. Many came from Great Britain, Ireland, and areas that are now part of Germany. Immigration increased in the mid-1800s, and again, many of the immigrants were from Northern and Western Europe. Many immigrants came from Ireland, where a disease was killing the potatoes, the most important food. The problem was so severe that it is called the Irish Potato **Famine** because so many people were starving. Many Irish people left their homes and moved to the United States.

After 1880, two things changed. First, the number of immigrants coming to the United States went up sharply. Second, many of the new immigrants were coming from different places—often from Southern and Eastern

Immigrants from Mexico

Not all of the immigrants who moved to the United States in the early 1900s came from Europe or passed through Ellis Island. For example, between 1910 and 1920, hundreds of thousands of Mexicans moved to the southwestern United States because of the Mexican Revolution. Many of these immigrants moved to escape the danger and lack of jobs this war was causing in Mexico.

Europe. At this time, people left places like Russia, Italy, and Greece in very large numbers. Immigration remained high until 1915, after World War I (1914–1918) began in Europe.

Why They Came

The millions of immigrants who left their homes in the late 1800s and early 1900s did so for many different reasons. Some left because they had

This picture shows Jews being attacked in Russia while government soldiers just watch. Because of these attacks, many Russian Jews came to the United States.

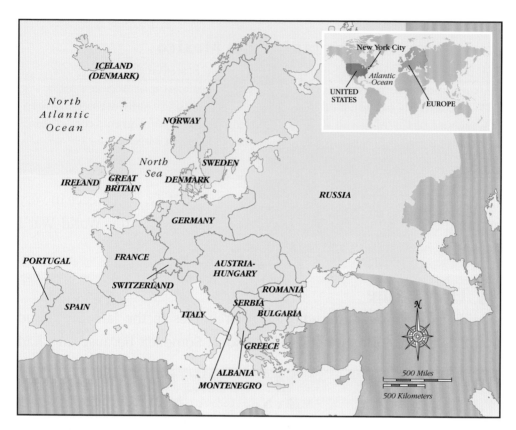

Many of the immigrants landing at Ellis Island came from countries in Southern and Eastern Europe, including Russia, Italy, and Greece.

problems with the government or wanted religious freedom. Others left because there was very little good farmland and very few good jobs. People could not support their families—or even get enough to eat.

In some countries, such as Russia, people were being forced into the army but did not want to go. In Russia and other places in Eastern Europe, Jews fled **pogroms**. Pogroms were organized attacks against Jews by gangs. The attackers stole belongings, burned homes, and killed innocent people.

People chose to move to the United States for many reasons. They had heard about all the opportunities. There was cheap farmland where a per-

In Their Own Words

Living Through a Pogrom

Fannie Kligerman told an interviewer about her life in Russia before she came to Ellis Island. She described a pogrom she lived through:

"But every night the pogroms were all around.... They were chasing us out. They were chasing after us, to kill everyone....How they frightened us.... One night we were hidden in a basement with a two- or-three-month-old baby. And we had to 'shush, shh, shh' the baby. We said, 'Keep still! Maybe somebody is going to hear us!' This I remember very well. We had working for us a [non-Jewish] girl.... While we were hidden in the basement, she gave us food through a little crack. I'll never forget it."

son could make a good living. Businesses were growing so fast that workers were needed in mines, factories, and all kinds of industries. People had heard stories of poor immigrants who had become rich by working hard in the United States. People believed they could make their dreams come true by immigrating.

The U.S. Government Takes Over Immigration

Until the late 1800s, the U.S. government was not involved in checking immigrants or controlling the number of people immigrating to the United States. Each state was in charge of admitting the immigrants who entered the country through that state. Most states did very little about them. New York City was the busiest port in the United States at that time, and many immigrants entered the country there. From 1855 to 1890, a total of 8 million immigrants went to Castle Garden on Manhattan Island. This was New York State's immigration station, and it was the busiest in the country.

A few states passed laws to control immigration. California passed a law to limit immigration from China. In 1875, the U.S. Supreme Court made a decision that California could not do that. The court decided that any state law to control immigration was **unconstitutional**, or did not follow the U.S. Constitution. Only the federal government could control immigration. The states continued to enforce new federal laws, but many of them did not do a very good job. In 1891, the U.S. government decided that it needed to have its own immigration stations to check arriving immigrants. Over the years, it opened stations in 30 cities.

The First Ellis Island Immigration Station

When the federal government decided to build a new immigration station in New York Harbor, some people wanted to build it on the same island

In Their Own Words

What They Left

Charles Bartunek was an immigrant from an area that is now in the country called the Czech Republic. He talked to an interviewer for a book about Ellis Island:

"We were one of the poorest families in the village…. We had a couple or three pieces of land that wouldn't amount to more than 2 acres all together [less than 1 hectare]…. My older sisters and brothers, they worked in the factory up there, making rugs and stuff for a few dollars. It was hard for us to get along…. In 1913, my brother Joe was scheduled to go into the army…. He was scheduled to report, but instead he and my brother-in-law left the country and went to the United States. They arranged things for us to come over to America. We sold what we had over there…. We came to this country in 1914."

where the Statue of Liberty stands. Many people did not like that idea. They wanted to keep the park that was around the statue.

Finally, a nearby island, Ellis Island, was chosen. A huge wooden building was put up. It looked like a big hotel on the outside. Inside it had a large room divided into narrow aisles by iron

Castle Garden, shown here, received immigrants landing in New York before Ellis Island opened in 1892. Some new arrivals wait outside with their belongings.

railings. It opened in 1892, but it was not well built. The doors did not open and close right, and the roof leaked. People who worked there were afraid heavy snow would cause the roof to fall in.

Then, early on the morning of June 15, 1897, a fire started in the kitchen. In three hours the whole building had burned to the ground. Nobody was injured, but the inspection of immigrants moved back to Manhattan for a time.

The Second Ellis Island Immigration Station

When the government rebuilt the immigration station on Ellis Island, the buildings were made of brick and stone so that they would be fireproof. The Main Building was larger than the old one. In its huge Great Hall, inspectors could examine 5,000 immigrants in one day. The building also had offices, rooms for private exams, and a dining hall. A laundry, hospital, and power plant to make electricity were also built on the island.

Immigrants who were steerage passengers, such as the people shown here, usually had an uncomfortable trip to the United States in the most crowded part of the ship.

in this way, because of someone's mistake. Sometime immigrants chose to make their names simpler, such as changing Finkelstein to Finkle or Stein.

Ships took three kinds of passengers: First Class, Second Class, and Third Class. Third Class was also called **steerage**. First Class was the most

In Their Own Words

A Rough Voyage

Arnold Weiss and his mother were in steerage during his 1921 trip as a child from Eastern Europe to Ellis Island. He told an interviewer about this trip:

> "We rode Third Class. I don't even recall the food I ate. Everything did not smell good to us because people were seasick…. I used to see my mother—she was green. I used to bring them [the seasick people] water; food they couldn't take…. I used to go up on deck and the storm on the sea used to wash me off. One time I almost went [overboard] because I did not weigh too much. I was just a kid…. We slept in bunks. There were three or four in a bunk and one next to the other."

expensive. Passengers in First and Second Class had their own rooms. Third Class, or steerage, was the cheapest but the most crowded way to travel. A ticket could cost as little as $10 dollars a person. Most immigrants were steerage passengers. The steerage section was at the bottom of the ship, near the steering equipment. Sometimes there were close to 200 people sleeping in the same room. The men slept in one section and the women and children in another. The beds were stacked two or more high. There were no windows or fresh air, and people were often seasick the whole trip. There was no place to clean up either, so the rooms often smelled very bad. The food for steerage passengers was not very good. Although the trip usually took about a week, it could take much longer if the ship hit bad weather.

When the immigrants reached the calm waters of New York Harbor, their worries did not end. Every immigrant knew he or she still had to go through Ellis Island.

Passing Through Ellis Island

S hips arriving in New York Harbor first stopped in Manhattan. There, the First Class and Second Class passengers got off. Inspectors checked their papers, and then these passengers were free to leave.

It was different for steerage passengers. They got off the ship and immediately got onto a **barge** or ferry for Ellis Island. These boats were very crowded, and people had their **baggage** with them. There were no seats, so people stood tightly packed together for the short ride.

The Medical Exam

Once at Ellis Island, the immigrants dragged all their baggage into the Main Building. Most left it in the huge baggage room, but some refused. They were afraid they would never see their things again and did not want to start life in the United States without the things they had brought. Then, a number was pinned to the coat of each immigrant.

Inside the Main Building at Ellis Island, all immigrants had a quick eye exam.

It was the number next to that person's name on the ship's manifest.

Next, all immigrants had to walk, single file, up the long staircase to the Great Hall. This was their first test. Health inspectors waited at the top of the stairs. The inspectors watched each person to see if he or she had any trouble climbing the stairs. If a person had trouble, a chalk letter was marked on the person's back.

Each immigrant then had a quick **medical** exam—often it was done in six seconds. A doctor looked at each person's eyes. This painful exam was done because some immigrants had eye diseases that could be transferred to other people. If it even looked like an eye might be infected or that there might be any other health problem, one or more chalk letters were placed on the immigrant's back.

Annie Moore (1877–1924)

Annie Moore traveled in steerage from Ireland with her two younger brothers. They were going to meet their parents in New York City. Annie turned 15 on January 1, 1892. On that day Annie became famous. She was the first person to pass inspection at the new Ellis Island immigration station. A statue of her is at Ellis Island, and another is in Ireland.

In Their Own Words

All Their Goods

Helen Barth worked for an aid society that helped immigrants at Ellis Island. She recorded her memories, and the recording is included in the Oral History Collection at Ellis Island. She described the new arrivals:

"Many of them [immigrants] came through with all their bedding and belongings and pieces of silver wrapped in a bundle. These were the last possessions they owned. Most of the children I saw were pretty shabby, clothing torn, and the mother would wear four or five petticoats because that was her baggage, you know; they wore everything they owned."

Immigrants crowd into the Great Hall, hoping to pass quickly through Ellis Island and be on their way to their new lives.

Many immigrants did not know when a mark was written on their back, but the people behind them did. They just did not know what the marks meant. When the people with a chalk mark were taken out of line and put into another line, everyone was upset. They thought this line was for those being sent back. What it really meant is that these people would get

Government inspectors asked certain questions of everyone trying to enter the United States.

a more complete medical exam in order to make sure their problems were not serious.

All immigrants then entered the Great Hall. Those with chalk marks were in one line; those without a mark in another. For many years the lines went between metal rails and there was no place to sit. Later, the rails were taken out and benches were added. On some days, thousands of people crowded into the Great Hall.

Inspectors Ask Questions

After passing the medical exam, an immigrant waited to see another inspector who would ask questions. An **interpreter** often helped these

Being Marked by Chalk

By 1917, doctors at Ellis Island looked for 50 different health problems. Their code included: B – back problems, E – eye problems, F – face problems, Ft – foot problems, H – heart problems, X – mental problems. Anyone with one or more letters written on his or her back had to have a more complete medical exam.

inspectors, since most immigrants did not speak English. The interpreters spoke English and another language. They **translated** the conversation between the immigrant and the inspector, so that each could understand what the other was saying. Many interpreters were immigrants who had already settled in New York. Sometimes there was no interpreter who spoke the language of the immigrant. Then the immigrant and the inspector had to try to understand each other as best they could.

Inspectors asked certain questions of every person. Some of the questions were about information that was on the ship's manifest. The inspectors would ask about name, age, hometown, the kind of work an adult had done, and where the person was going. They asked if the person had money and a job. Immigrants had to be careful about what they answered. The inspector had to make sure all adult immigrants could get a job if they did not have family, such as a husband, to support them. If a woman had traveled alone to the United States, the inspector had to make sure that someone was meeting her.

Most immigrants—80 percent of them—passed through Ellis Island easily and were allowed to go on their way. The rest were **detained**.

Immigrants who had to spend some time on Ellis Island were given free meals. This was often their first taste of American food.

In Their Own Words

Spending the Night at Ellis Island

Louis Adamic spent a night on Ellis Island in 1913. He wrote about his experience in his book *Laughing in the Jungle*:

"The first night in America I spent with hundreds of other recently arrived immigrants in an immense hall with tiers of narrow iron-and-canvas bunks, four deep. I was assigned the top bunk.... I had no bedding with me, and the blanket which someone threw at me was too thin to be effective against the blasts of cold air that rushed through the open window."

Being Detained

At Ellis Island, about 20 percent of the immigrants were kept on the island for many different reasons. Sometimes people had to stay because the immigration station was crowded and the doctors or inspectors could not see everyone that day. Those with health problems had to be given a longer exam. If the doctor did not feel there was a problem, the person got in line for the inspectors. If the doctor felt there was an illness that would soon clear up, the immigrant was sent to Ellis Island's hospital. Most people improved quickly and were not kept very long. Some had medical problems that needed a longer stay, while others had illnesses that meant they were sent back to the country they had come from.

If immigrants were detained because of non-medical problems, they had a **hearing**. A group of people called a Board of Special Inquiry met to discuss each immigrant's problems. This board had three immigration inspectors who listened to the case. Most of the time, the Board allowed the immigrants into the United States.

Women who were traveling alone were detained. They had to be met by a family member. If a woman was coming to marry someone, that man had to come to Ellis Island to meet her. Then, the man and woman were taken to New York City Hall and had to get married right away.

Immigrants who stayed on Ellis Island overnight slept in dormitories (often called dorms for short), which were large rooms with many beds. Food was served in a large dining room. Often, this was the first time immigrants ate American foods like ice cream and corn on the cob.

Rejected and Sent Back

Only about 2 percent of all immigrants were sent back to the country they had left. If a child was sent back, at least one older family member had to go, too. Sometimes a parent had to choose who would stay in the United States and who would go back to Europe. It was what everyone feared, and it was heartbreaking. Some immigrants went back to Europe and returned to Ellis Island later when their health improved.

In Their Own Words

American Food

In 1928, Vera Gaudits had been approved to enter the United States in Prague, a city in what is now the Czech Republic. She had traveled there from a farm in Estonia. She had to wait at Ellis Island until her husband met her. She described her time there—and her first taste of American food—to an interviewer for a book on Ellis Island:

"They gave us lunch—I never had a lunch like that before. It was a sandwich. We never had the [habit] in Europe to eat sandwiches. That was ham between rye [bread], I think…. I never saw a banana in my life, and they served a banana. I was just looking at it. And they [other immigrants] ate the banana with the skin on!… So when a Czech lady came a couple of hours later, I asked her what it was—the banana— and she showed me how to peel it and eat it."

Before leaving the Main Building, some people bought their train tickets to other parts of the United States.

Starting a New Life

Once immigrants were approved and could leave Ellis Island, they went through the Great Hall and back down the stairs to the baggage room. Some bought a train ticket or changed the money from their old country into U.S. dollars. Then they collected their baggage and took a ferry. One ferry went to New York City. Another went to the train station in Jersey City, New Jersey.

Some immigrants were met by a family member on Ellis Island or at the dock in New York City. A meeting point on Ellis Island became known as the "Kissing Post"—it was a place where husbands and wives, parents and children, friends and loved ones met, hugged, kissed, and sometimes cried tears of joy.

About one-third of the immigrants leaving Ellis Island stayed in or near New York City. The rest traveled to other parts of the country. Most of these people took the ferry to the New Jersey train station. Trains from there went all over the United States. Many immigrants were introduced to their new country by watching the cities and countryside go by outside the train's windows.

The Changing Roles of Ellis Island

For many years, Ellis Island was the busiest immigration station anywhere in the world. As more immigrants came, more buildings and inspectors were added. On one day in 1907, Ellis Island handled almost 11,500 immigrants—a record high number for a single day.

World War I Changes Ellis Island

In 1914, World War I began in Europe. Travel became more difficult and more dangerous, and immigration from Europe slowed down a great deal. Some immigrants still came through Ellis Island, but it was less crowded. Soon the government used it in other ways. During World War I, the government detained certain people on the island. For example, German ships were in New York when the United States entered World War I in 1917. Because the country was now at war against Germany,

In Their Own Words

Black Tom Explosion

On July 30, 1916, men working for Germany set off an explosion on the Black Tom Wharf in New Jersey. They wanted to stop the **munitions**, like gunpowder, stored at the Wharf from being shipped to the countries that were fighting against Germany. This dock was less than 1,500 feet (less than 460 meters) from Ellis Island. The blast was felt 90 miles (150 kilometers) away. At Ellis Island, 125 workers and 500 immigrants quickly left the island on the ferry. Frederick Theiss told Edward Corsi what happened:

> "The tide was coming in, and a west wind carried the fire toward the barges moored at the Black Tom Wharves. Suddenly I saw that the barges…had caught fire and were exploding as they drifted toward Ellis Island. Already the Ellis Island windows had been broken, the doors had been jammed inward, and parts of the roof had collapsed.

> "We thought for a while that the final explosion had occurred. Then we learned that the barges, which had floated against the Island and set fire to the seawall, were loaded with munitions…. Fortunately, the heroism of those who manned the tugs of the Lehigh Valley Railroad saved us. They towed the two flaming barges out to sea, where they sank amid concussions [blasts] which sounded like the end of the world."

the sailors on those ships were sent to Ellis Island. The government also detained people it thought were spies. At the same time, the Ellis Island hospital was used for sick and injured soldiers and sailors. Ellis Island was still a busy place.

In 1916, there was a huge explosion in nearby New Jersey. At Ellis Island, no one was seriously injured, but the buildings needed a lot of repair afterward. The Great Hall received a beautiful new tile ceiling, with thousands of tiles.

THE AMERICANESE WALL, AS CONGRESSMAN BURNETT WOULD BUILD IT.
UNCLE SAM: You're welcome in — if you can climb it!

This cartoon is meant to show how requiring immigrants to pass a literacy text helped keep people out of the United States.

Reducing Immigration

Most of the immigrants who came from Eastern and Southern Europe in the late 1800s and early 1900s were Catholic or Jewish, while most Americans at that time were Protestant. Most immigrants were poor but were willing to work hard for very low wages.

Some Americans were concerned that the large number of new immigrants would change American life. Some people were **prejudiced** against the newcomers just because they came from certain countries, had different customs and languages, or followed different religions. Some people were afraid there would not be enough jobs for all Americans.

For many years, some people wanted Congress to limit immigration. Congress had passed the Chinese Exclusion Act of 1882. It also passed laws to keep out people with certain problems and illnesses. Then, in 1917, a new law said immigrants had to pass a **literacy**, or reading, test. Each immigrant had to read to an inspector. He or she did not have to read in

English, but some immigrants had very little education, and they could not read at all.

Then, in 1924, Congress made major changes to the immigration laws. These changes limited the total number of immigrants allowed into the United States and also the number of immigrants from each country. The new laws allowed more immigrants from countries in Northern and Western Europe. Fewer people were allowed in from countries in Eastern and Southern Europe, Africa, and Asia. These changes slowed immigration to the United States.

Also, inspections were done in a different way. They were done before immigrants left a country instead of at immigration stations in the United States. There were U.S. government offices in just about every country. Most of what had been done at Ellis Island was now done at these offices.

In this photo from the 1940s, visitors arrive at Ellis Island to see people being detained there by the government.

Since fewer immigrants came to Ellis Island, the government used it as a detention center. People that the government did not want moving around the country were kept there. The United States fought in World War II from 1941 to 1945, against Germany, Italy, Japan, and other countries. The U.S. government kept about 7,000 people at Ellis Island. Some were Germans and German Americans who the government thought were helping Germany. Others were Italians and Italian Americans who the government thought were helping Italy. Ellis Island continued to be used as a detention center until 1954.

Ghostly Ellis Island

In 1954, the government closed Ellis Island completely. It tried to sell the island with its 33 buildings, two huge water tanks, and ferryboat. But many Americans became angry when they heard about selling the island. They did not want this symbol of American immigration sold.

For years after Ellis Island was closed in 1954, its buildings stood empty. After a while, some were in very poor condition. Their furniture and other things had been stolen.

Lee Iacocca (1924–   )

Lee Iacocca's parents were Italian immigrants. Lee's father, Nicola Iacocca, came through Ellis Island in 1902 when he was 12 years old. He worked hard at many jobs, even as a coal miner for one day. He saved his money, and in 1921, he returned to Italy to bring his mother to the United States. In Italy, he met Antoinette Perrotto and married her. He brought both women back with him. However, his wife had typhoid fever on the ship and lost her hair. According to the law, she should have been sent back to Italy, but Nicola convinced the inspectors that she had only been seasick. The family settled in Pennsylvania, where Lido Anthony Iacocca was born. Lido worked hard, went to college, and changed his name from Lido to Lee. He became an engineer at the Ford Motor Company in 1946 and was the company president when he left in 1978. He then joined Chrysler and saved that car company from going out of business. Later, he helped raise money to restore Ellis Island.

Lee Iacocca and his mother on a ferry to visit Ellis Island.

For 11 years the island sat empty. The buildings were falling apart. People snuck in and stole everything, from doorknobs to file cabinets. Vines grew through broken windows and trees grew everywhere. In 1964, one guard patrolled during the day and a guard dog was there at night.

Restoring Ellis Island

Then, in 1965, President Lyndon Johnson announced that Ellis Island would become part of the Statue of Liberty National Monument. The National Park Service would be in charge of it. The Park Service took off 40,000 bags of garbage. It fixed the seawall so the island would not wash into the harbor. From 1976 to 1984, the island was opened for limited visits. There wasn't much to see.

In 1982, President Ronald Reagan set up the Statue of Liberty-Ellis Island Centennial Commission. He asked Lee Iacocca to be in charge of it.

The restored Main Building reopened as a museum on September 10, 1990. As part of the opening ceremonies, 47 people were sworn in as U.S. citizens that day at Ellis Island.

September 11, 2001—Ellis Island Emergency Room

On September 11, 2001, terrorists flew planes into the twin towers of the World Trade Center in Manhattan. Nearby Ellis Island was used as a hospital emergency room. People who were injured were brought to the Main Building. Each injured person was checked, and those who needed more medical care were sent to a hospital. The National Park Service closed the Statue of Liberty and Ellis Island to visitors. Ellis Island and Liberty Island reopened in December 2001, but the Statue of Liberty itself remained closed until 2004.

Soon, the Statue of Liberty-Ellis Island Foundation was started. Its purpose was to raise money to restore both the Statue of Liberty and Ellis Island. It raised more than $500 million to restore these monuments.

The buildings on Ellis Island were in terrible shape. Fixing the Main Building became the biggest restoration job ever done on a building in the United States. It took eight years and cost $156 million dollars. The inside of the building was so damp that a heater ran for two years to dry out the walls. Everything needed to be cleaned, and missing things, like windows and pipes, had to be replaced.

The 1916 ceiling in the Great Hall was still in good shape, and only 17 of the 28,282 tiles needed to be replaced. When the paint was scraped away from the walls, workers found poems, drawings, and religious symbols drawn by immigrants. These were written using pencil or the blue chalk of the inspectors.

In 1990, the Ellis Island Immigration Museum opened in the Main Building. Since then, a few other buildings have been restored. However, all the buildings have been repaired enough so that they are not getting any worse.

Visiting Ellis Island Today

About 2 million people visit Ellis Island every year. Like the immigrants, visitors take a ferry to the island. Ferries leave from Castle Clinton. This was once Castle Garden, New York State's immigration center. An exhibit there tells about the Castle's history. Ferries also leave from Liberty State Park in New Jersey. The old train station there is where Ellis Island immigrants took trains to all parts of the United States. Before visitors board a ferry, they must go through a security check. These checks are done to protect special places, such as Ellis Island.

After a short ride, the ferry's first stop is Liberty Island. Then, the ferry goes to nearby Ellis Island. It stops in front of the Main Building. The Ellis Island Immigration Museum is in this building. Its exhibits tell about Ellis Island's role in immigration and tell the stories of the immigrants themselves.

Visiting the Immigration Museum

Just like the immigrants, visitors enter the Main Building through the baggage room. One part looks much as it did in about 1918, with piles of baskets and suitcases. Nearby, visitors can rent an audio tour and get tickets to tours, movies, and plays. The movie *Island of Hope, Island of Tears* is presented in two theaters, along with a talk by a Park Ranger. The back room is where railroad tickets used to be sold. This room is now used for an exhibit called *The Peopling of America*. It tells about the people of the United States and where they came from.

People visiting the baggage room can see how it might have looked when filled with immigrants' trunks, suitcases, and baskets.

The Island's History

Ellis Island has had different names and different owners. Native Americans called it Gull Island. The low island was mostly sand and oyster shells. Dutch colonists bought it from the Native Americans and called it Little Oyster Island. It was used for many things, and several pirates were hanged there. About 1774, colonist Samuel Ellis bought the island. In 1808, New York State bought it from his family and sold it to the U.S. government. The army built Fort Gibson on it to help protect New York Harbor. Later the military used the island to store bombs and gunpowder. This was all removed by 1890 when the government decided to build an immigration station there.

In 1834, New York and New Jersey signed an agreement saying that Ellis Island would be in New York State but the water around it would be in New Jersey. After 1891, the island was made bigger and two new islands were created. This was new land where there had been water. In what state was this land? Finally, in 1998, the U.S. Supreme Court decided that the original part of the island is in New York, but the 83 percent of Ellis Island that is human-made is in New Jersey. However, all of Ellis Island is owned by the federal government.

From here, visitors climb the stairs, just as arriving immigrants used to do, to the building's main floor and its Great Hall. A huge space, the Great Hall is set up with benches and the inspectors' tall desks. Along each end and on the second and third floors are more exhibits.

One exhibit, *Ellis Island Chronicles*, shows the story of the island itself. Another, *Through America's Gates*, tells what happened to immigrants at Ellis Island. The exhibit *Peak Immigrant Years* tells about immigration from 1880 to 1924. Many personal objects, photos, and papers that belonged to immigrants are part of the exhibit *Treasures from Home*. Many of these things were donated, or given, to the museum by immigrants or their families. There are several smaller rooms that show what it was like at Ellis Island in 1918. One is a room where the Board of Special Inquiry met. Sometimes actors conduct a hearing there so visitors can see what happened. Other rooms show where detained immigrants slept and ate.

Family Histories

In 2001, the American Family Immigration History Center opened. Here visitors use computers to search ships' manifests. These manifests are from the ships that came to New York from 1892 to 1924. Visitors can find specific people and get a picture of the ship they arrived in. Many visitors have located their ancestors among the millions of people who came through Ellis Island. This family history search can also be done over the Internet. In the center or from any computer, people can create an online family scrapbook to share with others. There is also an oral history room. People can record the story of their life as an immigrant or the stories of their ancestors. Visitors can listen to these stories here, too.

Visitors can see the Main Building as they approach Ellis Island by ferry.

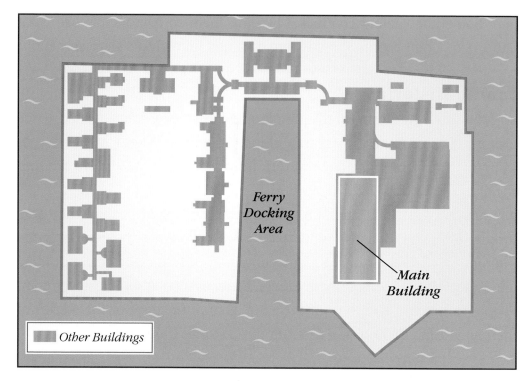

In all, there are 33 buildings on Ellis Island. Most of the exhibits for visitors are in the restored Main Building.

Wall of Honor

Behind the Main Building is the American Immigrant Wall of Honor. It is the largest wall of names in the world. In 2009, the names of more than 700,000 immigrants to the United States were listed on this wall. The immigrants do not have to have come through Ellis Island to be listed. They may have come before 1892, through another city, or more recently.

Other Things to See

There are 32 other buildings on Ellis Island. Visitors can tour the Ferry Building. It has an exhibit about the Ellis Island hospital. The other buildings are no longer falling down but cannot be visited. A new group called

This girl is examining some of the more than 700,000 names of immigrants to the United States that are on the American Immigrant Wall of Honor outside the Main Building at Ellis Island.

Save Ellis Island! is now working with the National Park Service. It is raising money and making plans to repair the rest of the buildings and use them for something special.

Visitors return to New York or New Jersey on the ferry. They will see, once again, the Statue of Liberty. They might imagine the relief that immigrants felt as they left Ellis Island and headed into a new life.

Immigration Today

American immigration is always changing. New laws change it. In 1965, Congress ended the limits on how many immigrants can come to the United States from each country. It has kept a limit on the total number of immigrants allowed in each year.

One of the exhibits at Ellis island includes photos of some of the many millions of people who have chosen to leave their native countries and try to make a better life for themselves in the United States.

The New Immigrants

In 2007, more than 1 million immigrants came to the United States. The four countries from which the greatest numbers of immigrants came that year were:

Mexico: 148,640 people   China: 76,655 people
The Philippines: 72,596 people   India: 65,353 people

Although immigration goes up and down, in recent decades it has been growing. In 1989, more than 1 million immigrants entered the United States, a higher number than in any year since 1907. Since then there have been several other years when more than a million people entered the country.

Events in the world change immigration, too. Immigrants still leave their **native country** because of war, or famine, or a lack of jobs, or a lack of freedom. But today's immigrants come from different parts of the world than the immigrants of a century ago. More immigrants come from Mexico than from any other country. Many immigrants come from countries in Asia, such as China, the Philippines, and India. Not as many come from Europe. Wherever they come from, the new immigrants, like the people who came before them, are hoping to find a better life for themselves and their families.

Ellis Island is a symbol to all Americans. It represents the hopes and fears of all immigrants, not just those who came through Ellis Island. It stands for everything that immigrants have to go through to begin a new life in a new country. It stands for the hope and the courage they have as they search for the American dream. As the Ellis Island Immigration Museum grows, it tells more and more of these stories.

★ **1774**	Samuel Ellis buys what is now called Ellis Island.
★ **1808**	New York State buys Ellis Island and sells it to the U.S. government.
★ **1811**	Fort Gibson is built on Ellis Island to help protect New York Harbor.
★ **1855–1890**	Castle Garden is New York's immigration center.
★ **1875**	The U.S. Supreme Court says that only the federal government can control immigration.
★ **1880s**	Immigration begins to increase as more and more people come to the United States from Eastern and Southern Europe.
★ **1892**	The Ellis Island immigration station opens.
★ **1897**	A fire destroys the buildings on Ellis Island.
★ **1900**	The rebuilt Ellis Island immigration station reopens.
★ **1907**	More than 1 million immigrants enter the United States through Ellis Island, a greater number than in any other year that the immigration station is open.
★ **1916**	The Black Tom Explosion in New Jersey damages Ellis Island buildings.
★ **1917**	A new immigration law says that only immigrants who can read will be allowed to stay in the United States. The U.S. government begins to use Ellis Island as a detention center.
★ **1924**	A new law limits immigration to the United States and says that immigrants must pass inspection in whatever country they are leaving. Immigration begins to drop.
★ **1954**	Ellis Island is closed.
★ **1965**	Ellis Island becomes part of the Statue of Liberty National Monument.
★ **1982**	The Statue of Liberty-Ellis Island Foundation is created to raise money to restore both monuments.
★ **1990**	The Ellis Island Immigration Museum opens in the restored Main Building.

ancestor: A family member who was born a long time ago, such as a great-grandmother.

baggage: What a person takes when he or she travel, usually suitcases.

barge: A large flat-bottomed boat that is used for carrying heavy loads. A barge often does not have its own power but is pushed or pulled by another boat.

detain: To keep from going away.

detention center: A place where the government holds people it wants to question, punish, or investigate.

famine: A severe lack of food, often caused by weather or war.

hearing: A meeting that allows facts to be presented to those in charge, usually before a decision is made.

immigrant: Someone from one country who moves to another country to live permanently.

immigration station: A place run by the government where people entering the country are examined to determine if they will be allowed to remain in that country.

inspector: A person who examines carefully.

interpreter: A person who listens to a speaker talking in one language and tells what has been said to someone in another language.

literacy: The ability to read.

medical: Having to do with health.

munitions: Bombs, bullets, guns, and other materials used in war.

native country: The country where a person was born.

pogrom: Organized attacks intended to kill or harm people in a certain religious or ethnic group.

population: The number of people who live in a certain place.

prejudiced: Having a bad opinion about a whole group of people without good reason or just because they are different.

restore: To fix something so that it is in its original form.

seawall: A wall built where land and water meet; it is used to keep water from flooding the land or land from washing into the water.

steerage: The least expensive— and least comfortable—section of a passenger ship.

symbol: Something that stands for something else.

translate: To change into another language.

transmit: To give or pass along to someone else, such as the germs that cause an illness.

unconstitutional: Does not follow the rules in the U.S. Constitution.

Read these books

Freedman, Russell. *Immigrant Kids*. New York: Puffin Books, 1995.

Hoobler, Dorothy, and Tom Hoobler. *The Italian American Family Album*. New York: Oxford University Press, 1998.

Peacock, Louise. *At Ellis Island: A History in Many Voices*. New York: Atheneum, 2007.

Sandler, Martin. *Island of Hope: The Journey to America and the Ellis Island Experience*. New York: Scholastic, 2004.

Thompson, Gare. *We Came Through Ellis Island: The Immigrant Adventures of Emma Markowitz*. Des Moines, Iowa: National Geographic, 2003.

Look up these Web sites

California Museum of Photography Ellis Island Exhibit
http://138.23.124.165/collections/permanent/projects/stereo/immigration/ellisisland.html#

Ellis Island National Monument Official Website
http://www.nps.gov/elis/index.htm

Immigration, Stories of Yesterday and Today
http://www.teacher.scholastic.com/activities/immigration/index.htm

Statue of Liberty-Ellis Island Foundation Official Website
http://www.ellisisland.org

Key Internet search terms

Ellis Island, immigration, New York City, Statue of Liberty

The abbreviation *ill.* stands for illustration, and *ills.* stands for illustrations. Page references to illustrations and maps are in *italic* type.

★ ★

About the Author

Hilarie Staton has written for students and teachers for more than twenty-five years. She enjoys researching and writing about history, especially using original documents. She lives in the Hudson Valley, an area where she finds many American history stories to tell. Other books about history she has written include *The Progressive Party: The Success of a Failed Party*.